Kids love reading
Choose Your Own Adventure®!

"I think these books are cool because you actually get involved with them."
Melanie Armstrong, age 12

"I think these books are great! I really like getting to be one of the characters."
Ahn Jacobson, age 11

"I think that this book was very exciting and it is fun to choose your ending. These books are great for all ages, too."
Logan Volpe, age 12

"I love the way that you can choose your own adventure and that the author makes you feel like you are the characters."
Shannon McDonnell, age 10

Watch for these titles coming up in the
Choose Your Own Adventure® series.

Ask your bookseller for books you have missed
or visit us at cyoa.com to learn more.

U.N. ADVENTURE: MISSION TO MOLOWA

BY RAMSEY MONTGOMERY

ILLUSTRATED BY WES LOUIE

CHOOSECO®
WAITSFIELD, VERMONT

UN Adventure: Mission to Molowa © 1995 Chooseco LLC,
Waitsfield, Vermont. All Rights Reserved.
Originally published as *The U.N. Adventure.*

Artwork, design, and revised text © 2009 Chooseco LLC,
Waitsfield, Vermont. All Rights Reserved.

Cover artwork © 2009 Chooseco LLC,
Waitsfield, Vermont. All Rights Reserved.

Illustrated by: Wes Louie
Book design: Stacey Boyd, Big Eyedea Visual Design

For information regarding permission, write to:

CHOOSECO

P.O. Box 46
Waitsfield, Vermont 05673
www.cyoa.com

ISBN-13: 978-1-933390-32-1
ISBN-10: 1-933390-32-8

Published simultaneously in the United States and Canada

Printed in the United States

0 9 8 7 6 5 4 3 2 1

BEWARE and WARNING!

This book is different from other books.

You and YOU ALONE are in charge of what happens in this story.

There are dangers, choices, adventures, and consequences. YOU must use all of your numerous talents and much of your enormous intelligence. The wrong decision could end in disaster—even death. But, don't despair. At any time, YOU can go back and make another choice, alter the path of your story, and change its result.

You are one of hundreds of kids who participate in the Model United Nations, a nationwide school club that acts out the international debates and decision-making of the real United Nations. Every year, the Model UN gathers in New York City to talk through the toughest decisions facing the world. You and your friend Achmed stumble upon a life-changing opportunity: to actually go visit areas of the world where these challenges are threatening people's lives and safety. There are several countries currently in crisis, and there's nothing you can do to prepare. What you must do now is decide: where in the world would you like to go?

Blinking your eyes, you try to filter out the bright lights shining in your face. One of many secret service agents motions you to the right. You follow his direction, taking your place next to three other students.

A roar of clapping fills the room. "This is it. I hope I don't faint or do something stupid," you tell yourself. In a few minutes you will be shaking the hand of the president of the United States in front of television cameras.

"Thank you, thank you," the president bellows into the microphone. "We must not forget that I am not the guest of honor today. That distinction belongs to these four fine students, chosen to represent our country at the Model United Nations."

The applause rises again as the president turns toward your group and waves you forward. Your legs feel as though they are made of lead, but you manage to stumble forward to the podium. Involuntarily, your hand reaches to shake the president's.

Moments later you and each of your fellow representatives brandish shiny commemorative plaques. The president rambles on with his speech, but you hear nothing. You stand mesmerized until somebody nudges your arm and escorts you from the building into a limousine. You can't believe you're on your way to New York City!

Turn to the next page.

2

The flight from Washington, DC, to New York is brief and uneventful. But once you get a view of the Manhattan skyline, you perk up. You are dazzled by the clumps of various buildings and bridges silhouetted against the clear blue sky.

As your limousine approaches the heart of New York City, you tilt your head back and stare up at the United Nations Building. The U.N. is an independent establishment—part of no country, yet belonging to all.

"Please follow me," a young guard in uniform calls to you and your three companions once you clear the security check in the lobby. "You're all expected in the General Assembly Room for a meeting with the other delegates."

Stepping aside, the guard opens a large oak door. You enter the monstrous room filled with about 150 kids approximately your age from all over the world. You look around in amazement. What strikes you first is the diversity of clothes the students wear and the languages they speak.

You notice a boy with a turban on his head and a long, flowing robe approaching you. He smiles. "You must be American," he says to your small group.

"Yes, we are," you answer.

Turn to the next page.

"Good, you can follow me. I'm from the United Arab Emirates. Our consoles are right next to each other," he informs you in a friendly voice, revealing a hint of an accent. "By the way, the name is Achmed."

You nod in agreement, and the four of you follow Achmed through the maze of the auditorium to a booth with a large sign on it. It reads USA. Taking your seat in the booth, you notice a pair of headphones. You grab them from their hook and put them on. Rapid Chinese enters your ears. You reach for a button, hoping to lower the volume. Instead you hear Russian, which you have spoken for many years with your grandparents. The voice tells you to address your attention toward the podium at the front of the room.

Go on to the next page.

Glancing up just in time, you see a man advance to the podium. You recognize him immediately. His name is Alphonse Gerhardt, and he is the secretary general of the U.N. You have seen him many times on television.

"Welcome to the Model United Nations." His voice echoes in everyone's headphones. "What you are all here for today is to get an overview of the U.N. and how it operates. Because there are so many delegates, we have divided you into small groups that will meet with me and others throughout the day. If you look in the folder on your desk, you will notice which group you have been placed in. It's a pleasure having you here. As representatives of the next generation, you are the future. Thank you." With a bow he leaves the room.

Removing the headphones, you open the folder and glance through it. You are in section M, a group of about thirty delegates that meets at 5:30, nearly six hours from now.

"Psst...," you hear from behind. Turning your head, you see Achmed smiling at you.

"What section are you in?" he asks.

"M," you whisper back.

"Me too. Let's get some lunch to kill the time."

"Sure—I'm so hungry. Airplane snacks are the worst."

"Would you like to try the food of my country?" Achmed suggests.

"Great, lead the way."

Turn to the next page.

A taxi takes you to a restaurant in a neighborhood about twenty blocks from the U.N. The sign above the door reads SALAAM. Sweet smells envelop you as you enter. You are led to a low table surrounded by large cushions.

"That girl over there"—you point carefully—"she was at the U.N. earlier today."

Achmed looks over at her and waves. "That's Benati. Her father represents the country of Burma, now Myanmar." He signals the waiter, handing him a small slip of paper.

Minutes later Benati approaches your table and sits down. Achmed introduces you. They order the meal, which is fine by you since you realize you can't read the menu.

Soon amazing plates of rice and meats are served. You can't believe how delicious each dish tastes. Suddenly you realize the time. The three of you settle the bill and rush back to the U.N. in a cab with only minutes to spare.

Dashing into the building and through the halls, you enter the delegates' lounge in the nick of time. You slide into a chair at a large oval table. Several minutes later, Secretary General Gerhardt scurries in with stacks of paper under one arm.

"I must apologize for my tardiness," he announces, straining to catch his breath. He sits down and arranges his papers on the table before him. "Events have arisen that commanded my immediate attention. They will now involve you."

Turn to the next page.

Gerhardt pauses, then continues, "There are two Security Council issues that require quick action. First, in sub-Saharan Africa, civil war has broken out in Molowa, a small country plagued with drought. The residents are fleeing their borders in masses, creating large refugee camps in the nearby Ivory Coast. Second, in what used to be the Soviet Union, a small independent country, Arkistan, is rumored to have gained control of nuclear warheads. A dictator, Nikolai Bolav, is now in control, and he threatens to use the weapons if he is not listened to.

"Two more issues have come to light. They are handled by the ECOSOC, short for Economic and Social Council. A U.N. expedition to the South Pole has been out of touch for three weeks. A rescue mission must be assembled. And a U.N. member working in remote Indonesia has discovered a small tribe living under Stone Age conditions."

General Gerhardt grants your section the task of creating committees to develop approaches to each problem. But first the members are to be divided up into two main groups: the Security Council and the Economic and Social Council.

If you would like to work on the problems in Molowa and Arkistan in the role of the Security Council, turn to page 33.

If you want to work with the ECOSOC in the South Pole and Indonesia, go on to the next page.

You're glad you have chosen to work on the Economic and Social Council issues. This branch of the U.N. deals with problems that range from teaching farming techniques in rural countries to monitoring trading practices between the Pacific Rim and the West.

"Let's check out the seminar about the team at the South Pole," Achmed suggests as the two of you walk down a long corridor.

"Sure. And the report about the Indonesian tribe takes place right after that," you reply.

Not too many people have chosen to listen to this problem. As you sit thinking about how lucky you are to be involved in such important projects, a tall man with flowing white hair enters the room.

"Hello, I am Dr. Octavius, the so-called resident expert on Earth's polar regions." His voice is soothing, and soon you find yourself leaning back in your chair, engrossed by his briefing on the crisis. The South Pole is an area of concern for the U.N. because it belongs to no single nation. Like space, it has been ruled that the pole is for everyone's use and cannot be exploited for its vast mineral reserves.

Go on to the next page.

10

Many countries have small, scientific bases on the ice cap, and the U.N. keeps a watchful *eye* on them. The missing U.N. team was monitoring other groups and conducting glaciology studies. Rescue attempts are costly and difficult, but it is the U.N.'s responsibility to secure the safety of its members.

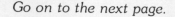

Go on to the next page.

"I'm hooked, Achmed," you say. "The poles are the planet's final frontier. I want to go to the Antarctic."

"Yeah, if you plan on freezing to death. Let's check out the lost tribe. Indonesia is warm and tropical," Achmed answers with a chuckle.

At the next meeting, a message is displayed from Professor Koa. It reads:

Buru, Indonesia—While hiking a nearby mountain in the jungle the other day, I came across a small tribe. They wear small loincloths and carry primitive spears and clubs. When they led me to their village, I realized that they are living in the ways of our Stone Age ancestors. They have few tools and live in caves. I would appreciate it if the U.N. could send a student support team to help me with the study.

Professor Lin Koa

Following this last meeting, a surprise announcement invites Model U.N. members to apply for these teams or expeditions. This is a once-in-a-lifetime chance.

"Let's sign up," you suggest to Achmed.

"Definitely—but for which one?" Achmed asks.

If the rescue mission to the South Pole sparks your interest, turn to page 12.

If you want to help study the "lost tribe", turn to page 16.

12

Steam rises from the Amazon jungle nearly twenty thousand feet below you as your plane heads for Tierra del Fuego, the southernmost tip of South America. Looking through the window, you are thrilled about the chance to see what Achmed calls the cold wasteland.

When the wheels of your plane touch down at the desolate airport, you wonder how you will get from here to the Antarctic. Between you lies the most dangerous stretch of ocean in the world: the Drake Passage.

"The weather is on our side. We can take a plane," one of your team members announces happily. "If the weather were bad...well, we'd be stuck."

At the far end of the runway sits an old twin-engine plane with skis instead of wheels. It's a DC-3, vintage 1940.

The chill of the polar ice cap penetrates the cabin as you cross the vast continent. Your destination is the Amundsen-Scott base, which lies directly on the pole itself, the only one out of thirty bases that does not lie on the coast. Through the white landscape you begin to make out the small buildings of the American base.

Snowmobiles rush to greet your plane as it touches down on the icy landing strip. At first you think they are just eager to see you. Then you notice the pilot emerging from the plane with a large sack of mail. You remember that sometimes weeks may go by at this outpost without contact from the outside world.

Turn to the next page.

14

Despite being dressed in a thick down parka, down pants, hood, gloves, goggles, and double-lined boots, you flinch at the biting Antarctic cold.

Everyone scrambles to escape the chill and enter the warmth of the base as quickly as possible. Once inside the huts, you exchange names. A woman named Elsse hands you a steaming cup of hot chocolate.

These were the first people to report loss of contact with the U.N. team. There are four of them, all meteorologists working on government grants.

"The U.N. team's base is about one hundred miles from here," Elsse tells you. "They set up a simple camp without any fixed structures."

"Have you made any attempt to reach them?" you ask.

"I'm afraid not. A severe storm has raged here for the last month. Today is the first day we have been able to see from one hut to the next," Elsse responds with a touch of regret in her voice.

After a large dinner, you spend many hours poring over maps of the area and making plans to set out in the morning. You will take three snow-mobiles and a large Sno-Cat. As you fall asleep, you relish the warmth of the hut, realizing that tomorrow night you will be sleeping in a tent out in the piercing cold.

Turn to page 20.

After you decide to work on the Arkistan arms crisis, you meet with seven other Model U.N. participants. Your group's discussion lasts for many hours. At last you are prepared to deliver your proposal before the General Assembly.

"Everyone ready?" one of the group calls. "Let's go!"

Moments later you march into the cavernous General Assembly Room. Suddenly you feel weak. In front of you sit important representatives from around the world.

"We the delegates of the Model United Nations," you begin, "have concluded immediate inspection of Arkistan is called for. The world must be put on notice that petty tyrants will not be permitted to hold the rest of humanity hostage to nuclear terror. We feel that a small force of U.N. specialists should travel at once to Arkistan."

Returning to your seat, you feel a wave of anxiety permeate your entire body. The room is silent except for the murmur of voices as the delegates discuss how they will vote. You stare at the large screen in front of you, awaiting the final verdict.

The YESes have it! Your group's recommendation is accepted! You are overwhelmed. It's an honor that these respected adults take your young group seriously.

Retreating to the cafeteria for a moment of thought, you sit at a table to eat your lunch. Alphonse Gerhardt slides in the seat beside you.

Turn to page 54.

16

As you emerge from the air-conditioned airport terminal in Singapore, the humid air smacks you like a hot, wet towel. You board a small train, and, looking at the view from your seat, you admire the glistening city.

During your flight you read about Singapore's history. Established by the British during the height of the empire to serve as a naval base and a military staging area, today it is an independent nation, a major economic center for the countries of the Pacific Rim.

Your journey to Buru has barely started. After a night's rest, you fly to Celebes. There you wait at a dock for an old mail boat that shuttles people and cargo to the islands of the Indonesian archipelago. Buru is one of its last stops.

The trip is long but fascinating. Small villages are snuggled up to the jungle forests, and crescent beaches hold clear, turquoise waters. The people seem friendly and welcoming to strangers. Finally you reach Buru.

"Welcome, I am Professor Koa," a wiry and wrinkled man says with a small bow. "Follow me. I've got a beautiful bungalow up on the hill."

Set on a cliff overlooking a crystal beach, the bungalow is neat and ringed by flowers—not at all what you expected to find in such a remote area. You are led to your room and find a huge bed draped with mosquito netting. Two large ceiling fans turn lazily to cool the room. You can't resist a quick swim in the ocean before you have to meet the professor in the dining hall.

Turn to the next page.

Achmed arrives while you are swimming and is already engaged in a lively conversation with the professor when you enter the dining hall.

"I guess you know Achmed," the professor says to you, motioning for you to sit down and join them.

"Call me Lin," the professor tells you. You like him already. He exudes warmth and curiosity. Lin talks about early tribal life—how some tribes were hunter-gatherers while others were farmers. This tribe seems to be a cross between the two. Lin believes they travel in a seasonal patterns. Firsthand observation of this tribe could be incredibly valuable to anthropologists.

"I'm leaving in the morning to visit them. I call them the Hidden Ones. I can take the two of you, but you may not get to meet them. Remember, you might frighten them. They're not accustomed to interacting with outsiders. The modern world is more of a nightmare than a reality to them."

"So maybe you should tell them about us first," you suggest.

"Yes, indeed, I will. But would you like to join me anyway? It might be a fun trip," Lin says.

If you choose to go with Lin in the morning,
turn to page 22.

If you think that it would be a good idea for Lin to warn the tribe about you in advance,
turn to page 26.

You realize that solutions to the ever-growing problem of the refugees can be found only in Molowa. After some discussion, Benati agrees. A man named Taenaq offers to help you on your journey into his native land. You, Taenaq, and Benati talk through the night about politics and hope.

"But rains are soon to come—and with them, hope of food and peace," Taenaq adds before heading off to his tent.

You leave as the African sun rises above the vast desert plains. The going is easy as you cross the border and enter Molowa. The roads are in fairly good condition. Yours is the only car traveling, but many campfires burn nearby. A steady stream of refugees journeys toward the Ivory Coast.

Rounding a clump of trees, Taenaq screeches to a stop in front of a roadblock.

"Everyone out. Hands in the air!" a man commands. One look at the machine gun in his hands is all you need to realize how serious he is.

Everyone moves to the side of the road. You boldly approach the man. "We are with the U.N. Taking us hostage would do your group no good."

Laughing, he answers, "We have no intention of taking you hostage. We only want your vehicle and supplies." With that, he jumps into your Jeep and drives off. You realize you are miles from anything, without food or water. You, Benati, and Taenaq join the weary refugees in hopes of making it back to the U.N. camp.

The End

The following day, snow sprays through the air behind you as you shoot across the white landscape on your snowmobile. You are bundled in many layers of clothes, but still you never feel warm. On the edges of the polar ice cap live penguins, seals, and other animals. But here, in the center of it all, only humans face the trial of the deep freeze.

You climb up a steep hill, then stop your snowmobile to look at snow, more snow, then some ice. Suddenly, with the shifting of a low cloud, you can see the camp across a crevasse. You wave frantically. The others soon join. There is no return signal from the camp.

"The camp is perched on the edge of a crevasse," one of the five expedition members observes. "We can't get to it from this side."

You see a wide crack in the snow right where the tents are pitched. As it moves, it sometimes splits open, forming crevasses.

"We must get to them as soon as we can," someone yells.

"Over there," you say. "I see a snowbridge."

Crossing it will be dangerous and difficult. Yet going around the crevasse might take hours. Helmut, the leader of your team, advises against crossing but puts the decision to a vote. It's a tie, except for your vote.

If you decide to follow Helmut's advice, turn to page 31.

If you choose to attempt crossing the snowbridge, turn to page 36.

You and Achmed decide to join Professor Koa. Even though you may not get to meet the Hidden Ones, it's better than staying behind, waiting for Lin to return.

The sounds of monkeys, parrots, and other birds and animals fill your ears. Everywhere you look you see only green. You can barely see the sky through the leaves.

"It was only three days ago that I last blazed my way through here," Lin tells you as he hacks away at the thick foliage with his machete.

Looking around, you realize how this small tribe has been able to remain hidden for such a long time. The island is so sparsely populated and covered by jungle.

"We are very close now. Their caves are in that hillside," Lin whispers, putting his finger to his mouth to signal you and Achmed to remain as quiet as possible.

Turn to the next page.

24

Walking on tiptoe, you sneak up to a small clearing where the muddy earth has been trampled by many feet. Glancing at Lin, you feel that something is wrong. Lin wanders over to the fire pit and sifts through the ashes.

"They're gone!" he groans, throwing the ashes to the ground.

"What do you mean? Will they be back?" you ask.

"No, I think we scared them. They must have gone deeper into the jungle to hide from us. It's obvious they're not interested in interacting with civilization. We must leave now."

Back at the bungalow you all decide that it's best to leave the tribe alone. Their world is very simple and peaceful. Perhaps contact with the outside world is not the best thing for them right now. Professor Koa seems very upset, but the last thing to do is insult or disrespect their way of life.

You stay in the bungalow for a week until the mail boat comes again. During that time you think a lot about the tribe and hope the exposure to civilization will not permanently harm them.

The End

After many exhausting hours of interviewing the refugees, you look for Benati. Several refugees hover around her, telling their personal struggles. They have left their homes and most of their possessions behind. Many have lost friends and family members along the way here.

"We are lucky we did not head off into unknown territory the other night!" Benati says as the two of you stroll toward the general operations tent to meet Omar Varsi, head of security for the camp.

"True. From what I've learned there are armed rebels swarming everywhere trying to find food. And they're not afraid to shoot!"

"We should get some kind of armed escort to protect us when we travel to Molowa," Benati suggests.

You think it's a good idea and decide to discuss it with Omar Varsi. You enter the large tent and find Omar wearing camouflage clothes.

"You are in luck. There's an armed troop transport due. You can ride with them," Omar promises.

"What?" you ask.

"In the morning," Omar replies.

During the night you and Benati meet with the men and women who will accompany you on the mission. The group of four is eager to get going, but you are all anxious about the unknown dangers. You keep up a constant chatter and exchange small, nervous jokes.

Turn to page 51.

"I'd feel more comfortable if they knew we were coming. I'm sure they're already confused about being discovered," you explain.

Besides, spending a few days at the bungalow is your idea of paradise. You and Achmed swim, snorkel, and dine on fresh fish. In the evenings you talk with the locals. You also spend time studying the culture and Lin's notes on the tribe.

"It's amazing that such a tribe has remained hidden for so long," Achmed muses as the two of you sit reading Lin's journal.

"With so much world travel, it's a miracle these people have avoided contact," you agree.

"Studying this tribe will give scientists and anthropologists insight into how our ancient ancestors lived. They will no longer have to rely on theories derived from archeological digs."

"The professor is returning tonight. We should prepare our gear," you comment.

"I just hope that he is still willing to take us to meet the tribe," Achmed answers.

Later that evening, Lin returns, bearing the news. "They are excited to meet us—they think I am a god figure sent to help them. We'll leave in the morning. Dress simply, take only a small pack."

Early the next morning the three of you set off on foot into the jungle. The trail winds through ravines with cascading waterfalls, then up steep hills of endless greenery. "Wait while I go ahead and let them know we're here," Lin says, heading down a narrow, inconspicuous path. You and Achmed remain in a small clearing.

Turn to the next page.

Within an hour he returns and explains that you must follow him as quietly as possible. As you progress single file, the foliage begins to diminish, and soon you find yourself entering a large clearing. A fire burns in the center, and around it sit about fifty people. One of them, probably a chief, rises and waves to you and Achmed. The people murmur animatedly.

"I use hand signals, noises, and simple drawings in the dirt to communicate. Why don't you give it a try?" Lin suggests.

You and Achmed approach a young boy with a long scar across his face. Through pointing and gestures you ask how he got the scar. He draws a picture of a ferocious animal in the sand. Though the conversation continues with great difficulty, you remain patient. You learn that his name is Kai and that he is very scared of something that he does not understand. When Kai fails to get this message across, he motions for you and Achmed to follow him to the top of the hill beyond the caves.

Turn to the next page.

Reaching the top of the hill, Kai scrambles up a tall tree. He motions for you and Achmed to follow. You carefully poke your head above the roof of the rain forest. You can see large plumes of smoke rising into the sky at some distance. The rumbling of the engines reaches your ears.

"Loggers! That's what's troubling him!" you shout angrily. "We must stop them before they get too close."

"Let's go and tell the professor. He'll know what to do," Achmed answers.

Back at the village you find Lin leaning over what appears to be a very sick person. "I fear that I might have infected them with a bacteria or virus against which their people have no immunity. It could kill them all, the way the American Indians and Eskimos suffered from contact with the Europeans."

When you explain about the logging, you realize how serious the threats facing the small tribe are. There must be something that you can do. Lin suggests that you take some blood samples to Singapore to have them analyzed. Achmed recommends figuring out a way to have someone else deliver the samples while the two of you handle the logging problem.

If you decide to take the medical samples to the hospital, turn to page 45.

If you choose to see what you can do about the logging, turn to page 39.

"I'm glad you decided to follow my advice," Helmut says to you.

You nod, preoccupied with the need to find an alternate route. You are fortunate the sun hardly sets on the South Pole at this time of year.

The journey to find a safe place to cross the crevasse takes the better part of the night. If you had had to travel under darkness, you surely would have frozen to death.

When you approach the U.N. camp you can see a figure jumping up and down to attract your attention. With a thrust of your hand on the throttle, the snowmobile jets ahead toward this lone figure.

"You are the greatest sight that I have ever seen," the person exclaims as you dismount your machine.

"We have been so worried about you—is everything all right?" you ask.

"Everyone is fine, luckily. The crevasse opened up in the middle of the night. Our communications shed and the tents with the food supplies and snowmobiles vanished," he responds as others begin to emerge from the tents.

Soon the Sno-Cat arrives. You manage to pack everyone inside and begin the trek back to the Amundsen-Scott base. Now things will return to normal. And so will your life—your mission is over.

The End

With your new friend, Benati, you leave Achmed to join twenty other delegates who have chosen to work on the Security Council problems. You meet in a large room behind a door marked SECURITY FORCES. Maps and computer screens displaying satellite images cover the walls, and a large flat desk in the center of the room lights up from an embedded computer—a smart desk.

"Pretty fascinating, don't you think?" a woman with long dark hair and dark-rimmed eyeglasses asks.

"I've only seen this in the movies," you reply.

"My name is Emilie Gonsales. I'll be showing you what is going on and everything we need to do regarding these two crises." Despite her relaxed manner and casual dress, you soon realize that she must be important.

When everyone is assembled, Emilie brings up a large map of Africa on the desk in front of her. It also projects onto a screen behind her. The scale of the map changes, focusing on the country called Molowa.

"Here it is. A nice, small, democratic country. But—and this is a big but—the rains have stopped. Drought—it's a killer. The people are starving. Warlords are taking over and stealing all the food and fuel. People are suffering."

"What can we do?" you ask.

"Difficult to say, but we need hard information. The Ivory Coast is swamped with refugees fleeing to their borders. They can't provide enough food and medical attention. Disease is rampant, and the camps are growing rapidly."

Turn to the next page.

"The U.N. will hold a conference at the Center for Refugee Affairs in Geneva, Switzerland. A peacekeeping force is on the agenda."

You and Benati exchange glances. "I can't believe they're letting us in on this," Benati whispers.

Before you can reply, Emilie continues. "The next situation is much more complex."

A map of Eastern Europe and what was formerly the Soviet Union flashes on the screen, along with a map of the Soviet Union before it broke up into many smaller countries in 1990.

"When the Soviet Union dissolved, nuclear weapons were left strewn about the many new countries. A U.N.–supervised disarmament of these weapons was enforced. However, recent rumors suggest that the country of Arkistan still holds a number of nuclear warheads. Arkistan's leader, Nikolai Bolav, is a ruthless military dictator. His government has denied possessions of these weapons, but pressure from the world's leading powers has forced him to admit a small team of U.N. inspectors."

When the lecture is over, you turn to Benati. "We have a chance to become involved in some major world issues."

"What interests you the most?" Benati asks.

If you choose to travel to Geneva and attend the conference on the Molowan problem, turn to page 47.

If you would like to learn more about the Arkistan arms crisis, turn to page 15.

You decide to take your chances with Aleksandr.

"So what's the next step?" you ask.

"I will come to get you tonight. Until then—just wait," he instructs before scooting out of your room.

Aleksandr's knock on your door comes in the middle of the night. It startles you even though you have lain awake for hours awaiting it. With a burst of energy you grab your backpack and open the door.

"We must move quickly. The guards are making their rounds and will be back in a matter of minutes," Aleksandr whispers as he leads you down a long corridor and out into a garden. The dark night makes travel difficult, and you bang into a car hidden by low-lying hedges.

"Yikes!" you yell.

"Quiet, fool, or we'll end up like pigs in a sausage factory!" Aleksandr snaps.

Your Russian isn't perfect, but you growl back at him, "Mind yourself, or heaven will call." It's an old Russian expression used by your grandmother, and it seems to have an immediate effect upon Aleksandr.

"Sorry. Get in the car. We're going to one of the safe houses where you can't talk with people who have seen the weapons that supposedly have been destroyed," Aleksandr confides.

The car careens down a narrow dirt road and slows near a cabin.

Inside, the cabin is small and dirty. You meet four men seated in chairs around a table.

Turn to page 43.

36

"I'll cross the bridge first—I'm probably the lightest," you offer.

"Are you brave!" Helmut says in awe.

When you reach the edge of the crevasse, you stare into the pit. The bottom is nearly three hundred feet deep. The snowbridge seems sturdy enough to support your weight, but everyone agrees that you will have to use the utmost caution.

"Here goes nothing," you say, putting a harness around your waist and clipping a rope into a carabiner.

Soon everyone is at work tying the ropes together and anchoring them to the Sno-Cat. You crawl across the bridge on your hands and knees, trailing the safety line behind you. The snow beneath you groans from the pressure that you put on it but continues to hold your weigh. With a great sense of relief you reach the other side and signal for the next person to cross.

Craaack! The crevasse suddenly widens! The snowbridge crumbles in front of you, leaving two team members suspended in midair. You drop to the ground and drive an ice ax into the snow. But the pressure is too great. You are dragged into the gaping hole. The rest of the team tumbles after you. There is nothing you can do as you plummet toward the bottom of the crevasse. It's a cold, permanent grave.

The End

"The loggers must be stopped! Is there another way we can get those samples to the hospital?" you ask.

"Actually, it might be faster if I go back to Buru myself and arrange an emergency plane to come and pick them up," Lin says.

After Lin leaves, you and Achmed head off toward the area of the loggers.

"They're going to strip the entire island," Achmed says in disbelief as the two of you look out over the jungle. "When the trees go, the tribe will surely disappear. They cannot survive in cities as we do—they have never even seen houses!"

What was once a lush rain forest is now nothing but destruction. The loggers have torn apart much of the landscape with their large machines. Tree stumps stick out of the muddy ground.

You descend the hill and set off across the ravaged land toward a group of men standing around a bulldozer.

"Who is in charge?" you ask in a barely controlled voice.

"Who wants to know?" a man wearing a hard hat answers with an American accent.

"The U.N.," Achmed replies. That seems to change their attitude.

"Come with me," one of them responds.

Turn to the next page.

40

You are led to a small, grimy trailer surrounded by a barbed wire fence. Sitting behind a desk is a large man smoking a cigar.

"Whaddaya want?" he growls.

"You must stop at once! You are invading tribal land," you insist.

"Are you out of your mind? Leave millions of dollars' worth of trees standing just so a few savages can live in peace?" he responds, stubbing his cigar butt out in a full ashtray.

"Come on, Achmed, this fool doesn't understand how important this tribe is," you blurt out. Your face is flushed with anger as you storm out of the trailer, slamming the door behind you.

Go on to the next page.

The next morning you return to Singapore and cable the U.N. Achmed remains with the tribe. The return cable asks you to plead the case in front of the International Court of Justice. Thirty-six jet-lagged hours later, you stand before the court.

"This tribe has as much right to their forest home as anyone does. We must fight to preserve this area for them. They represent much more than just fifty lives. If nothing is done to save them, an entire culture will disappear before our very eyes," you plead.

Silence follows your remarks. The U.N. is unable to stop the logging, and the delegates know it. Pressure can be applied, but the reality is that the loggers will have their way.

Now it is back to Singapore. Achmed meets you at the airport.

"I have a car waiting to take us to the corporate offices of the logging company," he says, helping you with your bags.

Once again anger flows through your veins when the president of the company tells you that he will not put a stop to the logging. He informs you that his permit gives him the right to the land regardless of who is living on it.

"You will regret this decision!" you yell as you storm out of the office. "We are going to stop them whatever the cost may be," you exclaim. Achmed nods in absolute agreement.

Turn to the next page.

42

You and Achmed discuss your options. You can try to get the Indonesian government to step in and help you, but this might take too much time. At the rate the loggers are working, it will be only a matter of weeks before they destroy the tribal land. Your other option is to sabotage their machines. This will put you outside the law—a crime, regardless of its motivation and purpose, but possibly worth it.

If you decide to try to get the Indonesian government to intervene, turn to page 68.

If you choose to sabotage the machines, turn to page 78.

"We paid a heavy price to get these," an old man chewing on a big wad of gum says with surprising vigor in his voice. He hands you a clump of photos and maps. "Use them well."

The rendezvous is short, and Aleksandr returns you to the castle. The photos and maps in your backpack seem to burn as though they themselves were radioactive.

"Stop where you are," a voice bellows from behind you. "Raise your arms and turn around."

Mission: unaccomplished. You are never heard from again. Your body is never found. The missiles and warheads find their way to aggressive small countries. Hopefully they will never be used.

The End

"I think the tribe's health is more important," you say.

"Good thinking. I'll arrange for you two to take the samples to Singapore," says Lin.

The medical clinic in Singapore is one of the best in the world. You hand over for analysis the samples of blood you obtained from the tribe.

With no business to attend to until the results come back from the lab, you and Achmed set off to explore Singapore. Originally designed as a fueling port for the British navy and merchant fleet, today Singapore is an independent leader in the Pacific Rim's economic world.

A note awaits you back at the hotel: COME TO THE CLINIC ASAP.

A hotel car drops you and Achmed in front of the hospital. You rush into the lab office. A team of doctors waits for you.

"This tribe has no immunity to modern illnesses," says one. "We will have to begin a process of immunization as soon as we can if we want to save them. It's risky at best."

Your heart sinks with the news. The immunization may be too late. Your only hope is that antibiotics may stave off death in these people.

With dismay you realize that it is now best for you to leave the tribe alone. They are in the hands of some of the best doctors in the world.

Returning to New York is disappointing, but you realize there is nothing more you can do.

The End

You decide to go to the conference on the Molowan issue and are pleased when Benati makes the same choice. You're headed for grand Geneva, Switzerland!

From the plane's window, you gaze down at the dark blue waters of Lake Geneva. At the shore of the lake you see a fountain of shooting water hundreds of feet into the air. Gently shaking Benalti's shoulder, you wake her. "Look out the window. Geneva is below us," you say.

"I can't believe how green it is. What a beautiful place," she says admiringly.

After a smooth landing, you are thrilled to finally check out Geneva. The flight was long, and the anxiety over the upcoming events has made you restless.

Emerging from the plane, you see a man holding up a card with your names printed on it.

"That's us," you tell Benati, pointing at the sign.

"Jolly good. I'm Niles Galbraith," a red-headed man says, with what you recognize as a British accent. "As soon as we have recovered your baggage, I will take you to your hotel."

With Niles behind the wheel of a sporty little convertible, you race through the maze of narrow streets. Niles explains that he is the director of the U.N. Commission on Refugee Affairs in Africa.

Turn to the next page.

"I'll be back at seven o'clock to take you to dinner. We have quite a bit to discuss. But now you should try to get some sleep and rid yourselves of the jet lag."

Once you are all squared away with your room, you find Benati and head out of the hotel. Jet lag or not, you are too excited to sleep now. Wandering around, you are amazed at how clean and orderly the city is. Feeling a pang of hunger, you can't resist buying a huge Swiss chocolate bar.

Back at the hotel there is a message at the desk requesting you and Benati to call Niles immediately. It is marked URGENT.

Go on to the next page.

As soon as you reach your room, you call Niles. "What's up, Niles?"

"Up until this point we have been in constant contact with our representatives in the capital of Molowa. That is, until yesterday," Niles responds.

"So, what's going on?" you ask.

"Intense fighting has broken out in the capital. Our contact was killed, and her partner fled in the U.N. Jeep to the Ivory Coast. This puts us in a dangerous position. The refugees are arriving faster than we can handle them, and we now have no idea what is going on inside Molowa."

"And you want Benati and me to fly there and investigate?"

"Yes. I'm flying to Abidjan tonight. We need to involve people your age now," Niles says in a serious tone.

You and Benati accept. After all, how could you pass up such an interesting and important task?

When you arrive in Abidjan, you smell the scent of no place that you have ever been before. It is both wonderful and fearful at the same time. From here you are picked up by a U.N. helicopter and flown to the area of the refugee camps that are growing on the border of Molowa and the Ivory Coast.

When your helicopter finally reaches the camp, your attention turns beneath you to the hundreds of tents and masses of people swarming around them.

Turn to the next page.

50

"I'll bet you did not imagine anything like this," Niles says as the chopper settles to the ground.

"I certainly didn't," you answer.

You are met by Dr. Harriet Stone. She leads you all to a large tent and explains that the great number of people arriving combined with the lack of food and medical supplies make a recipe for disaster. Death stalks the camps. Cholera, dysentery, and other plagues erupt with violence. "What the world doesn't see, the world doesn't care about," Dr. Stone comments. She seems exhausted.

"A major problem is that we have no current news from inside Molowa. We are cut off. We need someone to go inside and report back what is really happening. Perhaps even negotiate. We understand that at least five warlords and their followers are terrorizing people."

"I'll go, Dr. Stone," you say.

"I'll go, too," Benati chimes in. "But maybe we should interview the latest arrivals to better understand the situation."

"Well, time is crucial. But it's important for you to realize the risks involved. I leave it up to you to agree on a plan of action," Dr. Stone says.

If you decide that it is important to leave as soon as possible, turn to page 19.

If you think that Benati has a good point and choose to remain in the camp for a few days to conduct interviews with the refugees, turn to page 25.

Sitting in the driver's seat, you steer the four-wheel-drive Land Rover down a narrow road leading into Molowa. Benati sits next to you. Both of you are preoccupied with thoughts of what might lie ahead. The mere presence of the armed transport following you gives you a sense of security.

At noon you stop at a small village. Everything about it seems backward except for a neon sign advertising Coke. It is crowded with people on their way to the Ivory Coast. You learn that the area is controlled by a warlord named Kalarch, whose compound lies only fifty miles down the main road.

Three hours later you approach a roadblock. A guard jumps out in front of your Jeep brandishing a large machine gun.

"Who are you, and what are you doing here?" he shouts.

"U.N. peace mission," you say.

When you explain that you wish to speak with Kalarch, the guard disappears into his shack and picks up a radiophone.

"Kalarch has agreed to see you. But we will allow only three of you beyond this gate for the meeting The rest must wait here until the meeting is over," he announces when he returns. He keeps his Kalashnikov rifle at the ready.

Turn to the next page.

You gather your team together and discuss the offer. Splitting up would defeat the purpose of having the armed transport and put you in extreme danger.

"Maybe we should go back and wait for direct orders from the U.N.," Benati suggests.

"But we've already come this far. Plus, here's our chance to meet Kalarch," you point out.

"Well, I leave it up to you," Benati offers.

If you agree to Kalarch's demands and choose to take a small group beyond the roadblock, go on to the next page.

If you choose to return to the Ivory Coast, turn to page 61.

You, Benati, and a translator, Jamil, decide to meet with Kalarch. As you load supplies into your Land Rover, a man arrives on a motorcycle. "I will guide you," he says grimly.

"This could be crazy," you comment as the truck bounces down a rough dirt road. "We are walking right into the lion's den."

"True, but maybe we'll be able to help this poor ravaged country," Benati says.

"See that white chalky area over there?" Jamil asks, pointing. "That was once a great lake loaded with fish. Wheat and barley grew in the fields. Now there is nothing but death and suffering in the area."

What was once fertile grassland is now only a sun-baked earth. You had no idea the drought was this bad.

Ahead of you the motorcycle slows and pulls up to a large metal gate leading to an abandoned airport. Jamil tells you it has been unused since the Second World War. Once the motorcycle reaches a large building, you stop the Jeep and step out. Your heart pounds.

"Welcome to my humble headquarters," a small, thin man says, approaching. "I am General M.M. Kalarch. Call me M M. It is a great honor to have you here. We have been waiting a long time for help and guidance."

You attempt to hide your surprise. Such a warm welcome strikes you as odd and untrustworthy. You decide to play along. "I'm pleased you speak English. How can we help?"

Turn to page 59.

54

"I understand that you are fluent in Russian," he comments.

"Yes, my grandparents taught me," you respond between bites of your sandwich.

"Good. How would you like to join the team that we are sending to Arkistan? It's dangerous, but very important. I have checked your background. It seems for your age you are accomplished in many areas. We could use you."

You accept readily and are soon shuttled off to meet the other members of the team. They brief you on the situation in Arkistan.

Early the next morning you emerge from a small U.N. Learjet at the Tolstoy International Airport in Arkistan. A bearded driver meets you in a shabby, Russian-built Stoika sedan. Your destination is a medieval castle in the middle of a small village. It doesn't take long to reach it.

Turn to the next page.

"Let me get those bags for you," a boy about your age says in English as he approaches. He gives you a startled look when you respond in Russian.

"I'm Aleksandr, follow me," he says, leading you into the castle and up to your small, dark room. Pulling you close, Aleksandr whispers into your ear, "I am with the Arkistan resistance. We know why you are here. If you come with me tonight, I can show you some evidence that will prove the existence of the nuclear weapons and where they are hidden."

Turn to the next page.

58

You are stunned by Aleksandr's offer. This could be an incredible breakthrough before you've barely begun your mission. But bells go off in your head: It could also be a setup to get you expelled from the country and have the U.N. team discredited. Aleksandr could be a secret agent.

If you choose to wait until you have spoken to the U.N. team before going with Aleksandr, turn to page 72.

If you feel you cannot pass up this opportunity, turn to page 35.

"As you can see, we are suffering a great drought. We have little food or medical supplies. Many people were thrown out of their homes and their food was stolen. About three weeks ago, they started fighting with each other. This is what began the civil war," the general explains. "Supplies of food must now come from the outside. Many small warlords have been using the chaos to gain control over vast areas of land. I've been trying to keep peace, but attack is inevitable."

"So you aren't one of these aggressive warlords?" Benati asks.

"No, my friends. You see, I need to go to New York, to the U.N. Headquarters. I need to plead for my people," M.M. urges.

"Why should I believe you? There is a civil war going on, and you are a victor. What would the other nations have to say about this?" Jamil explodes in a flurry of questions.

M.M. smiles, remaining calm. "I represent the people of my country. Go into the towns and ask them about me."

You, Benati, and Jamil discuss the unexpected development. It sounds almost too good to be true. Maybe it's a ploy to lure you and outside help away from Molowa. Can you trust this man?

If you agree to take M.M. to speak at the U.N., turn to page 63.

If you do not believe M.M.'s story, turn to page 65.

"Prepare to turn around and get out of here," you whisper into the radio that connects you with the transport.

In the meantime, Kalarch's guard hurries back to his radio. From the excitement and the volume of his conversation, you sense that he's up to something.

"You will come with me now!" the guard suddenly announces, his face flushed and angry.

"Now!" you yell, jamming the Jeep into reverse. You speed down the road to the border with the transport close on your tail.

Benati points into the distance.

Dust from what look like trucks rises into the air.

"They're probably Kalarch's men. Let's hope we can reach the border before they catch up." You grab the radio to warn the transport.

Gunfire erupts along the road. Bullets rip into the Land Rover. A land mine explodes under you, shredding your front tire. As you spin out of control, you crank the wheel. The Jeep finally comes to a halt. You and Benati jump out and race to the nearby transport.

"Let's scram!" you shout.

Several miles down the road, the bridge you crossed only hours before emerges into your view. Now it's nothing more than a smoldering ruin. Men armed with guns and hand-held rockets line the side of the road. Your only alternative is to surrender.

Turn to the next page.

62

You realize now you should have taken the offer of entering Kalarch's camp. The group of gun-toting mercenaries forces you to a run-down building. You are separated from Benati and the rest of your crew. Several men lead you into a room not much bigger than a milk crate.

After two steaming-hot days locked in this room without food or water, you are barely coherent. You are dragged out and forced to sign a confession stating you are a government spy. You fear that if you don't agree to this, you will be killed. These men shoot at the drop of a hat. They want to gain control of the entire country and keep all the wealth for themselves.

They carry you back to the tiny room. Now you must wait to find out if you have made the right decision.

The End

You tell M.M. you will take him to the U.N. headquarters in New York.

"I'm delighted," he says, beaming. "There is now great hope for my people."

"Could you arrange to have a helicopter take us to the Ivory Coast?" you ask.

"All it takes is a quick call on the radio," M.M. says. In the meantime, you radio the rest of your crew at the roadblock, confirming your safety and giving permission for them to return to the Ivory Coast.

In the early morning you hear the whir of a copter's blades slicing through the air. A long flight leads to Abidjan in the Ivory Coast. After a rest, you board a flight for New York. The Security Council awaits your arrival.

At last you're back in the States. You and Benati escort M.M. Kalarch to a meeting of the General Assembly. This special session has been called to discuss the crisis in Molowa. After you, Benati, and the general offer your testimonies, the General Assembly votes. They decide that a U.N. peace-keeping force will be organized to reinstate the government in Molowa. It will also oversee the distribution of food and medical supplies throughout the country.

Turn to the next page.

64

Later, you and Benati are called into a small office where the Secretary General and M.M. Kalarch are seated.

"We want to thank you both for your courageous efforts to save Molowa," M.M. commends.

"It was nothing. We only did what we thought was right," you reply.

"Ah, but your intuition was remarkable. I would be honored to have you both come to Molowa as special consultants on youth matters, and help with the reestablishment of the government."

This is more than you ever bargained for—you can't pass up such an experience. Besides, it has to be more exciting than spending the rest of the summer in the good old USA!

The End

Not only do you not believe M.M., you think it's crucial that you escape soon. "M.M., I think Benati, Jamil, and I need to talk. Do you mind?"

"Not at all. You can find me in my office once you're done." He strolls back into the building, motioning to a guard to keep watch on you.

"We need to escape before we end up as prisoners. M.M. seems too eager to please. All his talk about helping the people of his country—I think he wants only to be made king. There is something funny going on here, and I don't want to wait to find out what it is," you whisper.

It doesn't take too much to convince Benati and Jamil. To avoid alarming M.M. and risking danger, you lie to him and agree to take him to New York. But you insist on waiting until morning to get a fresh start before returning to the Ivory Coast.

"Wonderful. I'm pleased you are participating in an even that will most certainly change the lives of my people!" M.M. exclaims.

Turn to the next page.

Late that night you, Benati, and Jamil gather your belongings and sneak out of the building. It is too risky to take the Land Rover, so you head off on foot. Fortunately the night is dark, and you are able to get away from the compound undetected.

After a safe distance, you stop and set up the radio, placing a call to the armed escorts for an emergency rescue. You agree on a time and place. Now it's time to make tracks!

The ground is hard, which makes the going easy. Soon you are near the road. But there is one last obstacle facing you: a river, skinny from drought but nevertheless the home of hippos. They are concealed by some straggly reeds as well as the darkness.

"Run for the trees!" Jamil yells. "Hippos!"

You turn and scramble for cover in a clump of trees. But you are too late! The charging animals attack. It's all over in less than a minute. Your corpses are never recovered.

The End

Though sabotage is probably what the loggers deserve, you decide against it. With the injunction from the U.N.'s Court of Justice in hand, you march into police headquarters. The desk sergeant is very responsive and immediately arranges for one of the police lieutenants to accompany you on your next visit to the logging company.

When you arrive in the lobby, the guards refuse you entry.

"This is our key to getting in," the lieutenant says, holding up his badge. "You can let us see the chairman or you can come down to the station with me."

The guards stare at each other and decide to let you pass. You are suddenly treated with respect as you proceed through the building. When you arrive at the chairman's office, he introduces you to his lawyer. During the talk, it is agreed that the loggers will not come anywhere near the small tribe. In fact, the loggers will cease logging once the current project ends. As you walk out of the building you feel tall and proud.

"I cannot thank you enough," Lin says when you return to the island of Buru. "In the meantime, the samples that we sent to the clinic were analyzed. The tribe is taking medicine for their illnesses and it looks like everything will be okay."

Turn to the next page.

You are elated to learn that the tribe is safe now. But the tribe has no immunity to germs that you and the others might carry. This was one of the major problems when Europeans first started coming to the United States. Many of the Native Americans died from minor illnesses. Hopefully doctors from Singapore will be able to prevent this from happening with the Hidden Ones.

In the morning, while you are sitting at the breakfast table in your bungalow, Lin comes to you with a look of concern on his face.

"I just received a call from the U.N. telling me to report to Papua New Guinea as soon as I can," he explains.

"What about us and the tribe?" you respond with a hint of disappointment in your voice. You have been looking forward to continuing your research on the tribe.

"My role in the U.N. is different from what we are doing here. They are sending in a team of specialists to work with the tribe."

You sit back and wonder why this has to happen just as things are starting to go well. The professor interrupts your train of though. "This work that I have in New Guinea is going to be very demanding. I would really appreciate it if the two of you would help me there."

"Where exactly will you be going?" you ask.

Go on to the next page.

"Investigating reports of oil and gas exploration and exploitation by foreign consortiums. It's an issue of concern somewhat similar to the logging problem. These consortiums frequently upset the rhythm of life with little or no benefit to the local people. Often this produces the so-called revolution of rising expectations, when modern civilization through radio, television, tourism, and business affects the indigenous peoples. The people realize and then crave what they do not have. Sometimes it is political, sometimes material. At any rate this is a time of great change throughout the world. I'd love for you to join. But I understand if you prefer to proceed with your mission here."

If you decide to remain in Buru to continue researching the tribe, turn to page 105.

If you choose to travel with Lin to Papua New Guinea, turn to page 95.

You don't feel prepared to risk taking up Aleksandr's offer. If you disappeared from your delegation, it might arouse suspicion about the role of your mission. If you were caught, you might face dismissal from the country—or even death. You send a message to Philippe Dumont, your mission leader, to alert him to your predicament. He agrees to meet with you in the study of the castle late that afternoon.

Entering the book-filled study, you confront a man waving what seems to be a wand. You notice Philippe sitting behind a large desk.

"What was he doing?" you ask Philippe, after the man leaves.

"Sweeping the room for bugs. He found four, placed here by the Arkistanis, in this room alone," Philippe says, holding up his hand to show you a small electronic listening device. He presses a button on a black metallic box. "This will take care of any other eavesdroppers. Now tell me what you've discovered."

"I think I've been contacted by the resistance movement. They claim to have the info we need. It could be a plant, however, designed to get us all in deep trouble," you reply.

"I can understand your hesitation," Philippe answers. "Even though we're a neutral organization, we often run into problems such as this. That Bolav fellow will do anything he can to prevent us from nosing around. The trouble is, we must know about those warheads. Sometimes we have to take risks."

Go on to the next page.

"What should we do?" you ask.

"Accept Aleksandr's offer. I'll fake your sudden departure from Arkistan due to illness. Then you go undercover. But if you're caught, you have no real protection. Will you do it?"

Without hesitation, you answer, "Yes. I'll do it."

"Good for you. Now here's the plan…"

The following morning you sit in a wheelchair at the boarding gate at Tolstoy International Airport. An attendant leads you down the ramp toward the 747 flight bound for New York and abruptly swings into a small room.

"Quick, change into these clothes," the attendant instructs, thrusting a uniform identical to his own into your hands. He removes his jacket and puts on yours. Then he sits in the wheelchair. "Hurry!" he says. "There isn't much time. Bolav's spies might be watching."

"Good luck," you say as you help him into a cabin-class seat. Then you leave the aircraft, pushing the now-empty wheelchair. You breathe a sigh of relief when you walk though the front doors of the airport undetected. You are now in a foreign country without a proper visa or passport. You will have to be very careful.

Aleksandr waits in a van in the parking lot with a change of clothes and false papers. He does not smile—for a young person he seems to have had a lot of experience in secret intelligence affairs.

Turn to the next page.

Aleksandr drives the van down to a waterfront crowded with large, abandoned buildings and then into a garage on the ground floor of a warehouse. Unknown people guide you to a ladder that descends into a hole in the floor leading to a subterranean chamber. You are overcome by a foul smell. A group of about seventeen people sit at a long table illuminated by one weak lightbulb hanging from the ceiling. The air is dense with smoke and fear.

"We in this room constitute the FRA—the Free Republic of Arkistan resistance forces. General Nikolai Bolav has come to power on the heels of the collapse of the USSR. His demented taste for murder and violence is unprecedented. He believes that he alone can rebuild the once-might Soviet Union. He must be stopped."

"We agree," you burst out. "The U.N. will help."

"Would you come with us now to take pictures of the weapons?" one of the members asks.

This would give you the proof you need. But it could be very dangerous. And you're not sure you can handle this task alone. It might be a good idea to contact the U.N. and see if they could send some kind of specialist to assist you. But by then it might be too late.

If you decide to go now and try to get the pictures, go on to the next page.

If you think you should request extra help, turn to page 79.

You remember Phillipe Dumont's words: "We have to take risks." So you agree to go at once.

Aleksandr hustles you into a separate room filled with clothes. He suggests you wear something comfortable since you will be traveling quite a bit. It takes you only a few minutes to grab a pair of thick wool pants, a cotton work shirt, and a sheepskin jacket.

"How do I look?" you ask when you emerge in your new outfit.

"Like you were born and raised in Arkistan." Aleksandr laughs. "But give me your watch. Nobody here has a watch with all those buttons."

You nod and hand over your watch. Then it's back to business. Aleksandr and you backtrack out of the tunnel to the van. Moments later, you pull up to a train station that resembles something from the early 1930s.

"Where are we going?" you ask Aleksandr.

"South, to the Malashin Mountains, where the FRA has its headquarters and training camps. Once we are there, we will get all the information and equipment we need to break into the weapons facilities."

"How come we seem to be the only passengers?" you ask after looking around the train.

Aleksandr explains. "When Bolav came into power, he made a rule that everyone had to carry a government identity card to travel within the country. These passes are very difficult to obtain because you must pass a security clearance."

Turn to the next page.

76

"Passes, please," the conductor interrupts.

This is it—I am doomed. Then, out of the corner of your eye, you notice Aleksandr taking two laminated passes out of his pocket.

"Thank you. You are lucky to be traveling to the mountains at this time of year," the conductor comments with a smile as he returns the passes.

"I told you we were well prepared," Aleksandr whispers.

The journey takes you through grassy farmlands, which remind you of the American Midwest. After many miles the train begins to climb the foothills of the mountains. Small villages pass by, and you being to wonder how much longer you will have to travel. When the sun begins to set, Aleksandr pats your shoulder and tells you that your stop is the next one.

The whistle from the departing train echoes behind you as you and Aleksandr approach a small white pickup truck on the road in front of you. This truck will take you into the mountains to meet the FRA.

Go on to the next page.

The truck ascends into the frigid mountains. You find yourself hoping the ride is over soon.

"We're almost there," Aleksandr yells, hid head sticking out the window.

In the valley below lies a tiny village, the mountain retreat of the FRA. As the van slowly winds its way down to the valley floor, you notice a series of light flashes coming from the hill opposite you. What does it mean? you wonder.

You soon find out. A man with a panic-stricken face runs from a house and yells, "Escape! Now! We are being surrounded. It's the army. Go back!"

Men in battle dress suddenly appear, firing at your tires. The van skids into a small ditch. Blood streams from the cut on your face.

"Hands in the air," booms a voice over a megaphone. Men swarm down from the hills and round up the entire village. Shots ring in the distance.

You are brought to a small room to await an interview. For many of the FRA their only interview will be with a gun barrel. Your time comes, and you are led into another office.

"We know who you are and what you were trying to do," an officer says.

"I'm with the United Nations. You must release me at once," you say defiantly.

"Correction. You were with the U.N. Now you are in our country without a visa and will remain here until our mission is accomplished." He turns. "Take this meddler away!"

The End

"I've decided," you whisper to Achmed. "I'm about to do something terribly illegal. If you want out, this is your last chance."

"I have come this far. I'm in it to see the logging end," he answers.

As planned, the two of you hide in the jungle near the loggers' camp before sunrise. In your backpacks you carry about a dozen bags of sugar, which when poured into the gas tanks of the bull-dozers and other machines will destroy the engines.

"Let's go," you say, crawling toward a big tractor. You climb up on it and pour a full bag of sugar into the gas tank. You and Achmed repeat this procedure until you have contaminated half the vehicles.

"I can't wait to see the expressions on their faces," Achmed whispers as the two of you sit in a large tree to watch. The sun begins to climb into the sky, and you see the first loggers emerge from their trailers.

Turn to page 83.

You decide to wait and discuss the opportunity with one of the U.N. delegates.

Sitting in a small café, you hope to bump into one of them. You know secret meetings among delegates are often held here. It seems to be your best chance of running into someone without blowing your cover.

After several hours and countless cups of coffee, you are about to give up when, amazingly, your friend Achmed appears in the doorway.

"Achmed, what in the world are you doing here?" you ask with excitement.

The color drains from his face as he replies, "I was sent to replace you. We all thought that you were sick back in New York."

"Quick, follow me. We must go someplace where we know that our conversation is private. I can explain everything," you whisper, grabbing Achmed's arm and dragging him out the rear of the restaurant.

In a small park, you sit down on a bench and explain your predicament to Achmed. "I really need some help. This mission is of the utmost importance," you tell him.

"I'll talk with Phillipe. He might be able to arrange something. Wait at the bench tomorrow morning. I'll make sure that someone is here to relay orders." Achmed leaves, and fear engulfs you.

You grab a bite to eat at a nearby kiosk and check into a cheap hotel. Fortunately, they do not ask for your passport.

Turn to the next page.

The next morning you approach the park bench with caution. Your heart seems to beat louder than a heavy-metal drummer.

Philippe approaches as you sit skimming a Russian newspaper.

"Good work. It appears that your information is accurate," he says in greeting.

"Great, but we need proof, and I can't do that alone. It's too much for me to handle," you answer.

"No need to worry. I've arranged for a specialist in cover matters to be flown in. He'll meet you here first thing tomorrow morning." Phillipe gets up to leave, then turns and hands you a small card. "Give this to him to identify yourself." On the card is a small picture of the Taj Mahal. "Remember, trust no one, believe nothing, expect the worst."

Go on to the next page.

The next day you approach the park bench once again. Assuring yourself that you're not under surveillance, you sit down. Suddenly a hand reaches from behind you and yanks you to the ground. A face, cloaked in a mask, glares at you. You reach into your pocket and pull out the picture of the Taj Mahal. The assailant loosens his grip on your arms and helps you to your feet. The mask drops from his face. "What was that all about?" you demand.

"Just checking to see if you were alert and ready for challenges. My name is Bjorn," he says in a stern voice. "If you are planning to undergo this mission with me, you must first pass a number of tests to prove that you are capable of handling what lies ahead of us. As I can see, you could use some work."

You're startled. This is your mission, and now this tough guy is making demands of you. Who does Bjorn think he is?

If you choose to put up with Bjorn's testing, turn to page 84.

If you decide not to accept his challenge, turn to page 87.

The big machines rumble to life and roll slowly toward the edge of the forest. Within moments the engines make clanging noises like metal knocking against metal. One by one they come to a halt. Angry loggers jump from their seats, bewildered at first, then aware of the foul play.

You raise your hand in the air with your fingers spread in a V for victory as Achmed claps you on the back. Mission accomplished.

The following night you return to the loggers' camp only to find that they now have guard dogs protecting the equipment. You grab your sacks filled with spikes and spend the entire night drilling them into the trees. When the loggers attempt to cut down the trees, the spikes will mangle their saws.

"Another few days of this and they will have no choice but to give up," Achmed says as you drive the last spike home.

Turn to page 86.

84

"Okay," you tell Bjorn. "I'll go along with your tests."

Bjorn glares at you as he talks. "I've set up a small outline for you to complete." With that, he walks away. On the bench next to you lies a manila envelope:

Travel by train from here to Ramnig.
When you arrive there, hike over the Sopis
hills to Bassa, where you will rent a car.
Drive to the airport. Buy a ticket to Molin.
In Molin, you will find a bicycle. Return to
this park on it under cover of darkness.

You stare at the note in disbelief. Is he mad? you ask yourself. But you decide to begin your journey as quickly as possible.

The following evening you return to the bench on a bicycle, weary from your long travels. Under the bench you find another envelope, which you rip open. Your anger rises.

You have completed the task. However,
you should have had the confidence to follow me without agreeing to this task. This
mission must go on without you. Take the
ticket enclosed and return to New York.

After a few minutes, your anger turns to relief that you are not going on a mission with a potential crackpot. You prepare to return to New York. Mission: unattempted.

The End

86

At sunrise you see two men carrying a large saw toward the woods. You hide in the bushes off to one side to watch. The powerful saw rips into the trees and bites into one of the spikes.

Scrocccch! The blade snaps and flings off into many pieces.

A burning sensation blasts through your leg, and you fall to the ground. A piece of the saw has cut deep into your thigh. At the sight of your leg covered in blood, you faint. When you regain consciousness, the faces of angry loggers fill your vision.

"Get me to a hospital," you yell to Achmed, before passing out again.

Weeks later you sit in your living room watching television. A piece about Indonesia catches your attention. The loggers have been stopped due to recent negative publicity. Your scheme of sabotage worked!

Your leg is still wrapped in bandages, but the doctors say that you will be fine. The tribe is now world famous, and their lands are fully protected. You, however, are still facing charges of malicious damage. Once your leg is healed, you will have to return to Indonesia to face criminal trial. Regardless of the verdict, you know you've done a world of good!

The End

"We have no time to waste on such tests," you tell Bjorn with conviction. "I am ready to go with you now!"

Nodding, Bjorn responds, "I like your spark, kid."

As the two of you leave the park, a gray van pulls up beside you, and the door opens. Bjorn jumps in, and you follow. Quan, the driver, introduces himself. He will act as the support team for you while the mission is in progress. With his long hair and small size, Quan does not look like somebody you would expect to be working with an elite undercover team. Bjorn tells you that Quan us the leading expert in communications, strategy planning, and computer technology, and most importantly, in finding escape routes.

As the van barrels down the highway, you are briefed on the mission. You will be entering the weapons facility and taking pictures of the warheads late this evening. Tomorrow you will return to the U.N. with the evidence.

"This is where we get out," Bjorn says as the van comes to a stop on a narrow dirt road. Bjorn carries a bicycle with him. "See you at the rendezvous," he yells to Quan as the van pulls away.

"The bike is part of the plan," Bjorn explains, responding to your perplexed look.

Turn to the next page.

Watching the taillights of the van disappear, you realize your mission has truly begun. There is no turning back now. Bjorn instructs you to hide in the bushes. He scurries across the road. You wait for a supply van headed for the installation to pass.

"If you have ever wanted to become an actor, here's your chance," Bjorn's voice crackles over your radio.

With haste you pick up the bicycle and steer it to the middle of the road. You lay it down and sprawl on the ground next to it. In the distance you can hear the rumble of at least one truck engine. You hope the driver will see you.

Turn to the next page.

90

Screech! Not one, but two trucks brake violently. The one in front stops only meters from where you lie. You hear excited voices and doors slamming. Several men run to check on you. When they reach you, they suddenly lose control of their muscles and slump to the ground.

"You didn't kill them, did you?" you ask Bjorn, getting to your feet.

"Of course not. I simply put them to sleep with tranquilizers." Bjorn laughs. "Here, help me drag them into the woods. You grab the keys from the second truck."

Minutes later the two of you climb into the cab of the first truck and take off, wearing military uniforms. A mile down the road, lights from the weapons facility light up the sky. Adrenaline pumps through your veins as you approach the gate. "I will take care of everything," Bjorn whispers as you slow to a stop.

Bjorn hands a folder of papers to the guard. He signs them and returns them to you, pointing to where Bjorn should park the truck.

Go on to the next page.

Bjorn maneuvers the truck near a large loading dock. You jump from the cab and head for the rest room that Quan showed you on the map. You wait while Bjorn follows orders.

Finally you hear two knocks. You open the door cautiously. Bjorn stands in front of you. Two unconscious men hit with his tranquilizer darts lie next to him. The two of you bind and gag them.

Following Bjorn, you sneak into the building and creep along a long, wide corridor until Bjorn motions for you to stop. A dense smell of cigarette smoke surrounds you. Three guards, playing cards, sit in a small alcove. In a flash, Bjorn draws the dart gun—ping, ping, ping!

"Where do you think…," the voice of one guard trails off. They are all out.

While you tie up the men, Bjorn places a small explosive device on the door at the end of the hallways. The two of you stand back. A puff of smoke rises and the door swings open. Beyond the door another corridor slopes downward at a steep angle. "Here, take this." Bjorn hands you the tranquilizer gun.

Slowly you follow him down the corridor to an elaborate steel gate. Bjorn prepares another explosive device and clamps it to the door. There is a small sound as the door yields.

The inhabitants of the control room are taken completely by surprise. Three men wearing lab coats recover their senses and charge you. You shoot each into unconsciousness.

Turn to the next page.

You fumble with your backpack and retrieve the camera. This is it—these pictures are the proof you need to condemn Bolav's corrupt government.

"Get a picture of the missile through this window," Bjorn calls to you from across the room.

"I can't believe it. That missile is powerful enough to destroy New York City!" you say in amazement, staring at the black and red missile snugged into it silo.

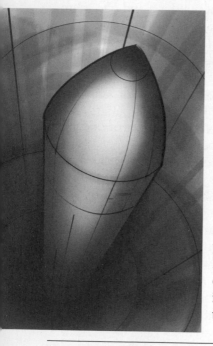

"You know what? I think that I can disarm these missiles," Bjorn says with pride in his voice.

"But we have to get out of here!" you exclaim.

"I know your mission is complete if you get those pictures. But I think we have a chance to do more than is expected of us. It's up to you," Bjorn says.

If you think it's worth the risk to try and disarm the missiles, turn to page 101.

If you decide the pictures are enough proof for the world to realize the threat of the missiles, go on to the next page.

"Let's just get out of here," you say.

Outside the building you turn to Bjorn and ask, "What do we do now?"

Bjorn replies, "That's why we have amazing Quan. He always finds a way to escape."

You scamper softly behind Bjorn into the forest, with only the faint moonlight to guide you. Infrared glasses stolen from the military base make your way clear. The glasses allow you to see almost as well as if it were daytime.

Suddenly you see the gray van in front of you.

"Stay here," Bjorn commands. Moments later he returns with Quan. "Get into this crate. We have to hide you since you have no papers. It will be sealed with the appropriate government tags. You're in for a long and bumpy ride, but it's your only chance to make it across the border to the nearest US consulate safely. From there you will return to the States and report to the U.N. Good luck!"

What seems like years later, you board a plane for the long flight to the U.S.A. Upon your landing, two men escort you from the plane to an awaiting car. You don't even have to pass through customs.

During the ride to the U.N., they ask endless questions about the weapons facility and what you might have seen that you did not take pictures of. Upon reaching the U.N., you are whisked off to meet with several members of the Security Council.

Turn to the next page.

"We have seen the pictures and read your report," an old man mutters. "Now tell us everything you know about Arkistan, its people, the government, and the infamous FRA."

It takes almost three hours for you to recount the whole tale. You are so exhausted that every bone in your body screams for sleep. You succumb.

"Wake up, you have been asleep for hours," your friend Benati whispers to you. "Welcome back. You're quite the hero. Stories have been flying around about you."

Before you have time to reply, a messenger arrives and relays, "You are wanted in room 301 immediately."

Four people face you in this small room. A tall woman speaks. "The Arkistanis have denied everything. They say that the pictures were fabricated. They are our only pieces of evidence—and we're not sure we can back them up. Are you willing to return with a small clandestine force to verify the pictures?"

If you ask to speak at the meeting of the General Assembly to offer evidence, turn to page 109

If you agree to return, turn to page 110.

Bidding farewell to these gentle people is tearful for all of you. Despite your excitement about the upcoming adventure in Papua New Guinea, you will miss these people.

"What exactly will we be doing when we arrive?" you ask Lin during your flight.

"The Darco Oil Company has been prospecting all around the island. Recently a team arrived and headed deep into the mountainous regions of the island. We believe that they may have stumbled upon something big. Oftentimes large multinational companies will try to hide any discoveries from local governments until they have been able to enforce contracts that benefit themselves and not the local population."

"How did they find out about this?" Achmed asks.

"Their government observed heavy air traffic into the region—helicopters, Helio-Station STOL aircraft, and other planes capable of landing in rough terrain. The government requested help when they ran into a hostile wall of denial that anything was going on. Darco does not enjoy a good reputation."

"So what do we do?" you ask, growing a little worried.

"We say we are from the ECOSOC, the U.N. branch that works with developing better living standards in remote areas like this. We're here to offer advice on crops, population, disease control. All perfectly true, only we gather information about them along the way."

Turn to the next page.

When you arrive at Port Moresby, the capital of Papua New Guinea, a U.N. Jeep is waiting for you on the dock.

"Let's hit the road. We've got a long drive ahead of us before we reach the foothills of the mountains," you say, jumping behind the wheel of the jeep.

The professor nods in agreement, happy that you have taken over the wheel.

The lush countryside is beautiful. Achmed reads through historical information about New Guinea. He explains that New Guinea was ruled by a U.N. mandate from the end of World War II until independence in 1975. Actually the U.N. only oversaw the northern part of the country, while the south remained under the control of Australia.

As you approach the mountains, you decide that you had better begin to act out your cover. You stop in a small village and inspect the entire place, taking lengthy notes and pictures. The professor guides the research, and the people you meet are amused by your questions and investigations.

A village elder tells you that a group of men has been exploring the area within an eighty-three-day walk from the village. He draws in the earth a symbol that resembles the logo of the Darco Company.

Go on to the next page.

Your drive into the mountains is delayed as you stop at several villages to gather more information about Darco. One of the villages lies quite close to a legitimate Darco operation. You are actually questioned by one of the employees and feel confident when the meeting is over that they believed your story.

The farther you travel into the mountains, the more rural the surroundings become. The road narrows into a bumpy track with grass growing in the center.

"We're not going to be able to drive any farther," you say, pulling to a stop in front of the wide river.

"No problem," the professor says, jumping from the Jeep and grabbing a large duffel bag. "Look at this."

He unwraps an inflatable raft. Moments later you finish filling it with air, using a foot pump. You load up all your gear and climb into the raft.

"This river will take us to within a few miles of where the Darco explorers are," Professor Koa informs you.

Turn to the next page.

As you float down the river, you listen to the sounds of the jungle. It's a medley of bird and animal calls. Suddenly you hear a large rumbling roar. The raft begins to rock.

"Paddle over to the side of the river. We are approaching a large waterfall!" the professor shouts. All three of you work vigorously at the oars. You manage to maneuver the boat safely to the riverbank.

Go on to the next page.

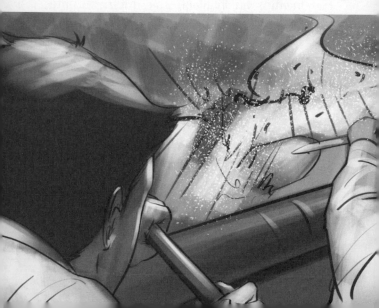

After a sigh of relief and a short rest, you begin to unload your gear. You will have to carry the raft around the waterfall. Achmed wanders into the forest to explore a bit before you set off again. He returns breathing hard.

"When I got to the top of the ridge, I could see smoke rising in the distance. I think that it's coming from the camp of the explorers," he reports.

Turn to the next page.

You quickly deflate the raft and hide it in the bushes. Lin estimates it's about five miles to the point from which the smoke rises. You decide to set up camp and make your appearance in the morning.

By sunrise, you're on the move.

"We have got to be close now," you say, hacking at the vines with your machete.

You follow the smoke trail to a small clearing with a group of tents. Several men stand around a small fire drinking what appears to be coffee from metal cups. You approach.

"We're from the U.N. We're doing research on villages in the area. Maybe you can help us."

"No villages here," one of the men announces in a harsh voice. "Last village we saw is about fifty miles east."

"So what are you doing here?" you ask.

"University group. Studying the flora," a small, dapper man responds without a flinch or a smile. "Why not have lunch with us?"

Lunch is pleasant enough but doesn't offer you any insightful information. Spotting an exotic butterfly, you excuse yourself and head toward the jungle. You pass a tent where a man bends over a radio speaking in rapid-fire Arabic mixed with English.

If you decide to remain where you are in hopes of deciphering the topic of conversation, turn to page 108.

If you decide to fetch Achmed, turn to page 115.

"All right—let's give it a try. But—but how long did you say the tranquilizers will last?" you stammer. You feel nervous about being so deep in enemy territory.

"About three hours," Bjorn answers. He goes through the pockets of the scientists, pulling out a ring of keys. "Go and stand guard by the door. Use the radio set if you need me."

You sit anxiously by the door, staring at the clock in front of you as the precious minutes tick by. You can't help thinking about the unconscious guards.

"Bjorn, it's been over two and a half hours since we fired the first shots. Let's get out of here," you plead into your radio.

"Just one more warhead to disarm."

Nearly thirty minutes later you finally see Bjorn running toward you.

"Hurry. Some of the people are starting to come to. We need to get out of here!" Bjorn rushes past you, pushing the door open.

You spring through the corridor and manage to exit the building without anyone seeing you.

"Quick, to the gate!" Bjorn calls, his breath short.

Seeing guards at the gate with guns at the ready, you freeze.

"Break for the docks! There's no time to reach Quan," Bjorn hollers. You scram.

Turn to the next page.

"There's a small fishing village only a few miles away. We'll go there and escape by boat into the Baltic Sea."

You continue running through the forest. The muscles in your legs and arms burn. You can't keep up with Bjorn. Above the loud beating of your heart, you hear the noise of dogs in the distance—they must be tracking you! You get a burst of energy and push your legs to quicken your pace.

The moon glimmers on the water ahead, and you sprint as hard as you can for the doors. Bjorn is already standing on the deck of a small fishing boat and starting the engine. It roars to life as you jump on board.

As the boat races out into the harbor, searchlights stab in the dark. You realize the patrol boats can move much faster than your boat.

"Quick! Over the side with the firing mechanisms!" Bjorn yells.

You open Bjorn's backpack and dump the firing mechanisms in to the water, desperately hoping you make it into international waters before they catch up.

"Stop your engine or we will fire!" booms a loud voice over a microphone.

You look up to see the military helicopter hovering above you. This is it. You have to surrender. You and Bjorn look at each other, sweating from exhaustion and regret as men rappel down from the helicopter and arrest you for espionage.

The End

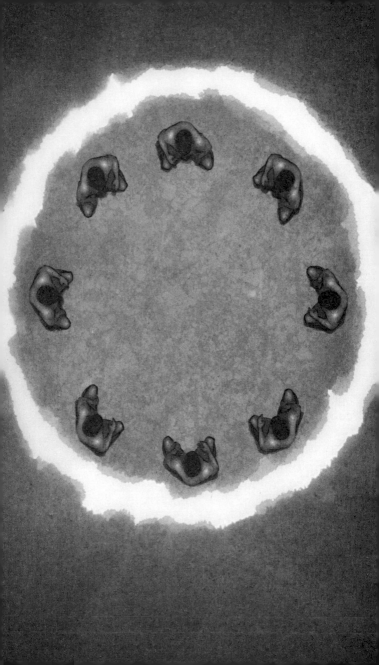

With the arrival of the specialists, your small bungalow overflows with anthropologists from all corners of the globe. It upsets you that Professor Koa has left, but you realize that there is much you can learn from these people.

Achmed has decided to stay as well. Both of you will act as guides to the tribe's remote village. You are somewhat hesitant to bring other outsiders to them. You fear for the corruption of the tribe's simple and peaceful way of life.

It has been a while since you last visited the Hidden Ones. Everyone in your group is very eager to see these simple forest dwellers.

When at last you reach their village, the tribe is gathered in a circle. An intense humming sound—like hundreds of hives of bees—greets you.

"This must be some kind of religious chant." Achmed observes.

"I believe you are right," one of the anthropologists comments. "We are fortunate that they feel comfortable enough with us to let us hear their sacred chant."

Finally the humming ceases, and you move forward carefully to introduce the newcomers. The chief pulls you aside and explains in sign language that this is a ceremonial day celebrating the birth of their tribe from Mother Earth. Tonight there will be a great feast celebrating their creation. You are all invited to join.

Turn to the next page.

You and Achmed are the only ones who choose to remain with the tribe for the night. The others are wary about imposing. While you set up your tent, you notice five tribe members slipping off into the woods. "What do you think they are doing?" Achmed asks.

"Judging by the fact that they all took spears, I would guess that they are going to catch the dinner for the feast."

This makes you a little tense; you have seen the tribe eating roots and vegetables, but you have no idea what else they might serve you.

As the sun sets you are led to the top of a nearby mountain, where a large fire burns. You sigh with relief when you see that they are cooking fish wrapped in leaves. You are embarrassed to admit that you had feared they would be preparing something too exotic—such as monkey.

When everyone has been served dinner, the humming chant begins once again. People get up and dance around the fire in undulating rhythm. One member of the tribe approaches you and takes your hand, leading you into the circle of dancing. You dance through the night.

As the sun begins to rise, you are motioned to the center of the circle. The chief announces that you are now a full member of the tribe. You will always be welcome to join them here in their rainforest hide-away. What an honor! Even more outstanding than meeting the president of the United States, you think as you fall asleep in your tent.

The End

108

Hiding behind a large tree, you eavesdrop, hoping to catch a few words of English. The waiting pays off. You hear several phrases in English, and the words "spy" and "death" ring out clearly. You're in for it, and you know it.

Your pulse beating uncontrollably, you retreat as quietly as possible. No good. The man jumps to his feet, dropping the radio.

"What are you doing here?" he asks furiously, staring straight at you.

"I chased a butterfly into the forest and wanted to get a picture," you answer defensively, holding up you camera.

"A likely story, but you need not worry about us. We will be leaving in a few hours. You will have plenty of time to find your hidden village or butterfly or perhaps oil," he replies, getting up and stomping toward the clearing.

Time to escape, and you know it. Back at the clearing, you give the professor and Achmed the sign to leave. Amazingly, no one prevents you from going. But when you reach the waterfall, you find your raft slashed to shreds. Ahead lie countless miles of jungle slogging.

That's when you first hear it: a strange metallic clicking. Sure enough, it's the unlocking of the safety on an automatic weapon!

"No! Don't fire!" are your last words ever.

The End

When you enter the General Assembly, you are once again amazed at how many people, all from different countries, gather here to vote on a common issue. Alone, no nation could bring together such a consensus, but here every country has a say. And though each country has several delegates, it has only one vote.

The meeting is long and tiring. The Arkistan representatives continue to deny that they have any weapons in their country. You rise to the podium and present your statement. Afterward the delegates break for recess.

It is decided that the U.N. will send its forces into Arkistan to inspect the compound where you took pictures. Furthermore, economic sanctions will be brought against Arkistan until the crisis is resolved. Arkistan will not be allowed to buy or sell any good from countries within the U.N. community, a measure that will result in great shortages in the small country. You and the others hope this economic pressure will be sufficient; a military answer is the last desirable of all and will be prevented if at all possible.

The End

Across the Atlantic once again! You arrive at night at a darkened airfield in an unknown country. An elderly woman picks you up in a beat-up car and drives you to an old farmhouse, where you meet with General Simoline. He wears no identification on his uniform. This is truly going to be a clandestine operation. You wonder if the U.N. is even involved!

Only miles away lies the Arkistan border.

"You'll parachute from a plane with a group of four others. They are all specialists. You will take them to the nuclear facility," the general explains.

"But I've never parachuted before," you exclaim.

"No need to worry. We have the best instructors in the world. They will train you," the general replies.

Before the sun rises, you are awakened and led to a large plane.

An instructor in battle dress, wearing a parachute, says, "It is very simple. You just jump through that door when I tell you to. The chute will do the rest."

You spend the entire day in practice and instruction. You gain confidence as the hours progress, but fear still gnaws at you. "I wish I were back home!" you keep saying to yourself.

Turn to the next page.

112

Word that the Arkistan government has denied any involvement with nuclear weapons spreads through the lines like wildfire. The General Assembly decides to increase its force. Time to go! Your team suddenly increases from four people to over one hundred! Armed intervention is dangerous and implemented only as a last resort—but this situation has become desperate.

Ahead of you awaits the plane, revving its four massive engines. You feel sick with fright.

"Here, put this on your face and hands," a woman tells you, holding out a tube of black grease. "When you jump in the night you want to blend in with the sky."

The plane ascends to almost six thousand feet. As it levels off, you notice the yellow light flashing. Members of your crew begin to rise and prepare for the jump. You adjust your parachute and wait for the light to turn green.

Sweat streams down your face as you try to remain calm before the light turns. With a flash it is green, and you leap from the plane with the others. You are sailing through the sky when you realize what is truly happening. What will it be like when we land? Will the opposition be waiting for us? you wonder as your chute opens.

Go on to the next page.

As you drift toward the ground, you see a small meadow, where you decide to land. A gust of wind embraces you and propels you toward a line of trees. There is nothing you can do as the branches catch you and leave you hanging several feet above the ground. From the pocket in your pants you pull out a knife and cut yourself free. You fall to the ground.

Dazed, you lie under the tree and let out a huge breath. After a quick check, you learn that no bones are broken—you have suffered just a few minor scrapes and bruises. You glance at your compass and refer to your map. The rendezvous point is about a mile away. You get to your feet and begin walking. Remaining in the shadows as much as you can, you listen for the sound of the enemy— but you hear nothing.

Turn to the next page.

"How was the jump?" one of your team members asks, rolling up her chute as you approach the meeting spot.

"Great. Had a little trouble with the wind at the end," you reply.

"You may not be the only one to run into difficulties tonight. I just got off the radio with command and learned that Arkistan ground forces know we're coming. There's a leak somewhere. Be ready for anything."

Once everyone arrives and the supply chutes are retrieved, you all load your packs and set off for the compound. The scouts meet you on the trail and inform you that tanks are surrounding the entire area. This leaves your group with a tough choice. You can attempt to knock out the tanks with your hand-held rocket launchers—but this would be an act of war—or you can have some of your forces create a diversion while you lead a small team into the compound.

If you choose to lead a small team into the compound, turn to page 117.

If you think you have a better chance of success with a frontal assault, turn to page 118.

Tiptoeing backward, you sneak back through the forest into the clearing. Achmed is talking with one of the researchers. You explain that you need help with your pack to get him away.

"One of the men is in the forest talking in Arabic over the radio. I don't trust him. I need you to listen to what he is saying," you tell Achmed as you lead him into the forest.

When you are near the tent, the two of you crouch low behind a tree and listen to the conversation. After about fifteen minutes the man slams down the radio and heads back to the clearing. You remain quiet as he passes.

"We are up against some tough operators," Achmed whispers. "They have found vast oil reserves and a huge deposit of titanium. They also suspect that we are here to spy on them."

"We have to warm the professor and get out of here!" you cry.

"Not so loud! I did not tell you the worst of it. They think that we are from one of their rival companies. That they to 'get rid of us,'" Achmed murmurs.

"Let's not waste any time!" you say, nudging Achmed to follow you back to the clearing. Luckily you find Lin alone.

Go on to the next page.

116

When you explain your discovery, he brushes it off lightly. "Just continue to tell them you're with the U.N. Besides, I'm sure they're afraid to do anything harmful."

"I disagree. The man was serious when he spoke those threatening words. These men are ruthless. I'm not taking any chances," Achmed says with conviction.

"Well, you both have been making the right decisions so far. What do you want to do?" the professor asks you.

If you decide to stick around and hope the men believe your cover, turn to page 121.

If you choose to escape as soon as possible, turn to page 122.

You select a small group of paratroopers to help penetrate the compound. In the meantime, a separate force will create a diversion to enable you to enter the compound undetected.

With several others, you crouch in the forest waiting for the sound of gunfire. The shots will signal that the diversion has begun.

"I hope they fall for it. All of the tanks must be on the other side before we can make our move," one of your team whispers.

"They will. Listen—the tanks are starting their engines," you assure him.

As the sound of gunshots gets louder and louder on the opposite side of the compound, you observe the tanks near starting to move away. Loud explosions indicate that your forces are successfully destroying the tanks.

"This is our chance. Let's go!" you yell, running through the dense foliage.

Turn to page 119.

118

While your companions prepare weapons for the frontal assault, you meet with the commander. The two of you go over the floor plan of the building and where you should focus the attack. Since ground forces have been detected along the border, the only support you will get will be from two gunship helicopters. These helicopters carry enough missiles and guns to extinguish all the tanks. What started out as a reconnaissance mission is turning into something more than you bargained for. The U.N. tries to avoid force, but sometimes it is justified. Still, force isn't always a surefire solution.

With the sound of the whistle still ringing in your ears, you and one hundred other paratroopers begin the assault. Bullets fly over your head, and missiles streak toward the tanks as you move closer and closer to the building. You see tanks blown apart before your very eyes. You continue forward. Suddenly you notice a breach in the defenses and make a break for it.

A bullet finds its mark—and you are it. The mission is a success, but you don't survive to enjoy it.

The End

As soon as you are out of the forest, you drop to the ground and crawl toward the fence. Wire cutters do their job, and soon all of you are inside the compound. A guard blocks the entrance, but he is soon immobilized.

"Hurry! They'll only be able to keep up the diversion for so long!" you shout to the others as you enter the control room.

The scientists stare at you in disbelief. One of your team moves them all into a corner, using a gun as a threat. Several shots erupt in the room.

Then the firing ceases. The smell of gunpowder is acrid and frightening.

It takes eleven minutes to wire the entire room with bombs and take more pictures of the nuclear weapons. When the bombs go off, the entire building will collapse, destroying the nuclear arsenal without activating the warheads.

Turn to the next page.

120

Quickly your team evacuates the building, along with the scientists. Moments later the building erupts in a brilliant flash. You hope no lives are lost on either side, but this is an unfortunate risk that has to be taken.

Weeks later, the resistance movement launches an all-out attack on Bolav and his men. After a fierce and bloody battle, the FRA triumphs and Bolav is imprisoned. Your role has been important, but only a rare few will ever know about it.

The End

"I'm for staying here," you reply. "But I'm going to straighten these people out first."

"I really wouldn't do that," Achmed warns.

But you ignore him. You glance at Lin to see his reaction—he's speechless. Summoning all the courage you can muster, you march over to the group of men sitting around the fire.

"We need to talk," you say determinedly.

"Oh yeah—about what?" one responds.

"We know who you are and what you are doing. You can forget about the university act."

"Watch out!" yells Achmed.

One of the men pulls a gun from behind his back and chides, "Then I guess you will have to forget everything."

"You are mistaken," you assert. "We are with the United Nations under orders or the government of Papua New Guinea. If you harm us, you will never make it out of this country."

You look around and see the shock on their faces. They never expected your boldness.

"All we want is for you and your company to negotiate contracts fairly before mining for titanium and oil. This country deserves a share in the profits," you say with confidence.

After a long discussion, they offer to take you with them to Port Moresby in their helicopter and help negotiate the mining rights.

When the agreement is finalized, you feel a sense of pride. The profits the government earns help improve living conditions in remote villages scattered about the island.

The End

"Let's get out of here," you plead.

As fast as you can, the three of you gather up your belongings and dash into the forest.

"We managed to get out in the nick of time," you comment, pointing to a helicopter in the distance. "Let's hope they don't anticipate our next move."

"Traveling by this route will take us much longer, but we cannot risk being detected on the river," the professor observes, looking intently at a map.

The trek through the jungle takes almost three full days before you reach a remote outpost. There, you locate a radio and contact the U.N. to notify it of your desperate situation. A helicopter is on the way.

Go on to the next page.

In New York you report before the General Assembly about Darco's illegal operation. An extensive investigation is launched, and ultimately Darco is barred from conducting any further business in New Guinea.

Your performance is well noted, and the U.N. is eager to involve you in future expeditions. For the time being, however, you will eagerly accept Achmed's invitation to stay with him in the United Arab Emirates. After so many weeks of furious activity, you could use the rest.

The End

CREDITS

Illustrator: Wes Louie was born and raised in Los Angeles, where he grew up drawing. He attended Pasadena City College, where he made a lot of great friends and contacts, and then the Art Center. Wes majored in illustration, but also took classes in industrial design and entertainment. He has been working in the entertainment industry since 1998 in a variety of fields.

Ramsey Montgomery
1967-2008

Ramsey Montgomery was an explorer of the world. He loved to meet new people and cultures. Although he passed away at age 40, he managed to see much of the world in that time. In his adventurous life, he lived in Vermont (where he was born and grew up), Colorado, England, New Mexico, California, Thailand, and Vietnam. He visited so many places that the list would be too long to include. Ramsey loved to ski, hike, and bike, but his true love was reading. He read widely and deeply. Ramsey will always be missed by his family and his many, many friends from around the world.

Visit us online at CYOA.com for games and other fun stuff!